THE WELL-ADJUSTED TOURIST
Presents:
YELLOWSTONE COUNTRY

THE WELL-ADJUSTED TOURIST
Presents:
YELLOWSTONE COUNTRY

A HANDBOOK FOR HOW TO TOURIST GOOD IN YELLOWSTONE'S EASTERN CORRIDOR

THE PARK COUNTY TELEGRAPH

gatekeeper press
Columbus, Ohio

The views and opinions expressed in this book are solely those of the author and do not reflect the views or opinions of Gatekeeper Press. Gatekeeper Press is not to be held responsible for and expressly disclaims responsibility of the content herein.

The Well-Adjusted Tourist Presents: YELLOWSTONE COUNTRY: A Handbook for How to Tourist Good in Yellowstone's Eastern Corridor

Published by Gatekeeper Press
2167 Stringtown Rd, Suite 109
Columbus, OH 43123-2989
www.GatekeeperPress.com

Copyright © 2022 by The Park County Telegraph
All rights reserved. Neither this book, nor any parts within it may be sold or reproduced in any form or by any electronic or mechanical means, including information storage and retrieval systems, without permission in writing from the author. The only exception is by a reviewer, who may quote short excerpts in a review.

The cover design, typesetting, and editorial work for this book are entirely the product of the author. Gatekeeper Press did not participate in and is not responsible for any aspect of these elements.

Library of Congress Control Number: 2022935621

ISBN (paperback): 9781662926921

For Wyoming.
Long may she live.

CONTENTS

Foreword ix

Tiny Chapter 1: Welcome, Warriors ... 1
   The Telegraph 2
   How to Read This Handbook 4
   Tough Love 7

Tiny Chapter 2: Cody-Your Likely Home Base 12
   Other Towns in the Basin 15

Tiny Chapter 3: Recreation and Whatnot 18
   Hiking 18
   Biking 22
   Trail Rides and Drives 27
   Fishing 29
   Camping 34
   Yellowstone 40

Tiny Chapter 4: Other Activities 48

　　Sleeping Giant Zipline.................. 49

　　Guns and Such 51

　　Stampede............................... 55

　　Museums............................... 58

　　River Rafting 63

Poorly Defined (and drawn) Things 68

Worthless Maps 80

JANKY games 86

Acknowledgements 90

FOREWORD

Hi there.

My name is Pete and I *currently* (will explain) live in Houston, Texas. (Don't stop just yet, it will all make sense shortly)

I'm one of the guest writers mentioned in this handbook although "great" as it relates to my writing is just wildly overstating the matter. Maybe my kids will get a laugh out of reading that when I'm gone so I won't protest for precision's sake.

You see, I had the absolute privilege of getting to live in Cody for a few years with my wife and young children.

Northwest Wyoming is every ounce as spectacular as this book says it is unless your preferences lend themselves to endless sprawling concrete, more cars than wildlife, and smog.

Of course that's not you or you wouldn't have read this far...or maybe you're a glutton for punishment...I really don't know.

Wyoming is awesome, especially the Northwestern quadrant. I've hiked it, biked it, visited Yellowstone multiple times, skied at Sleeping Giant (kids first learned to ski here at 3 and 1 y/o), enjoyed many of the museums cited, gone rafting, celebrated the Fourth of July downtown, and **DEFINITELY** fished the area. OMG the fishing...it is spectacular. Not "yay I got a bite" spectacular, but "OMG is that a rainbow trout or baby tarpon" spectacular. I'm comparing it to all sorts of places I've fished including Colorado, the Gulf Coast, and others.

The people are also amazing. I happen to consider some of the area's inhabitants some of my very favorite people and dearest friends. I mean that, and I'm a cynical dude.

The best and final mic-drop endorsement I can give this place is the stated admission that I am not really a "tattoo person" but the day before I had to leave I got my first ink. It was/is "82414", otherwise known as the zip code of Cody, WY. I am unapologetically biased, but with mileage to back it up. Oh yeah, bear spray…have some around.

And finally, the "currently living in Houston" part. As much as The Telegraph politely discourages everyone from moving here en masse, I plan to eventually. Tough gravel nuggets Telegraph.

TELEGRAPH ENTRY, 9/23/21

Yellowstone Announces New Park for Reckless Idiots: YOLOstone

Leaves are turning and tours are leaving- such is the cycle of another successful tourist season in our beloved Yellowstone National Park. Solid visitor numbers confirm 2021 was an encouraging year for the park, COVID be damned. With the large number of normal, law-abiding tourists, statistics also show a steady ratio of idiots are certain to follow. And follow they did.

Determined to make the best out of the worst, a special panel put their heads together on a plan to keep normal visitors in the park, and draw those whom seek injury and lawlessness to a new, more appropriate venue. Meet YOLOstone.

'YOLOstone has everything an idiot would want for their vacation: bears to taunt, bison to ride, walkways to ignore…only in a new area where they won't be bothered by the normal folks who just want to take pictures and buy expensive souvenirs.'

Park officials are ecstatic, and may even make YOLOstone a new observation point for normal people who have the curious desire to see a person gored. I mean, who hasn't caught themselves watching a few too many YouTube videos of tourists being gored?

Exactly. See you at the YOLOstone observatory, peeps. Here's to 2022!

TINY CHAPTER 1

WELCOME, WARRIORS

Well. You did it. You booked your trip to **Yellowstone** country. Or maybe you're already here. Maybe you're just thinking about it. Maybe you picked this small book up for levity. Education, even.

Whatever the reason. Good on you and welcome to **Wyoming**- if it has or when it does happen. This small, snarky handbook will walk you through a few things to make your trip even more enjoyable. It isn't gospel. It's not completely factual, either. In fact, it is mostly opinion with a little experience thrown in. Take from it what you will, but at the very least consider that what you are reading could be a tiny bit insightful. We're grateful you purchased it.

Oh- and if you stole it, you had better plan some good deeds on your vacation.

THE TELEGRAPH

Before we really dig in, what exactly is **The Park County Telegraph**? Think of us as the collective personality behind the greatest community on earth...manifested in the self-loathing form of satire. Why satire? Perhaps the great Charlie Chaplin put it best,

"Syd, I love this country. I owe it everything. That's why I can make fun of it!"

Just substitute *county* for *country* and your name for Syd's.

Lizz Winsted also said,

"Good satire hopefully provides thought-provoking conversation."

So you see, **The Telegraph**'s satire is really just a weird love language. And we love it here. Plus, how else could you try and give justice to Kanye's fleeting ranch ownership, south of Cody?

'We' is used a bunch. While there are a couple hidden contributors to our regular blogs (for both an expansion of talent AND a shield to hide behind should things get too controversial), it's largely just me. A 40-year-old native in the midst of the dream. I sourced a bunch of great writers for this book, whom I will attempt to give full justice and credit to, throughout.

Back to 'We.'

This handbook is a first for **The Telegraph**- a commitment to follow through on a silly but ambitious project (some three years in the making. Okay, like a year and some change, but still). May it pay homage to the area we call home, and make you laugh a bit in the process. Check out The Telegraph on our website, Facebook or Instagram.

Thanks for reading. Truly.

HOW TO READ THIS HANDBOOK

Read this thing with a light heart. Laugh a little and remember- don't take yourself too seriously during the process. Enjoy the overabundance of choppy, broken sentences, and poor attempts at levity, too.

For the do-it-yourselfers, this book should serve to get you off on the right path towards a host of activities. For those of you looking to maximize each experience, consider this book as a handshake with some local businesses who really know their stuff.

Each chapter will highlight a couple things we believe are worth knowing, along with a **Semi Pro Tip** or two that will make you just a little bit better than your peers for knowing. We've thrown in some fake articles from the annals, too. Because we're funny.

The Telegraph is guessing you are in the area to see Yellowstone.

Sweet. **Yellowstone** is phenomenal and ironically, there isn't a whole lot about the place in this little book. That's because you probably know what you want to see in the park and how you intend to make that happen. It's also because, let's be honest, after a couple days there, you will have seen most of the features on a typical checklist. Sure there'll be some tips and tricks for maximizing the **Yellowstone** experience, but just know the primary focus of this guide is to enjoyably occupy all the other awkward gaps on your vacation.

The information herein isn't exhaustive, but should serve as a compass to get you pointed in the right direction to enjoy your interests more efficiently. Pun intended. There is no substitute for learning face-to-face, so many chapters will list businesses or guides who can assist you even better than **The Telegraph**. Guided activities can get pretty expensive, but they are well worth it- especially if your only other option means doing it all on your own.

As an editor's note, the businesses mentioned in this handbook are not associated with The Telegraph. Or vice versa. We've just used them before and can stand behind an endorsement.

Further, most chapters will highlight ways you can either get hurt or irritate the locals while recreating. Incidentals, but you endeavor to be a well-adjusted tourist, right? We add them because we love **YOU**.

TOUGH LOVE

Here's the deal. Tourism is a major industry in this neck of the woods. Your dollars go a long way toward providing for local businesses. We think it's even fair to say that some folks make the majority of their living during tourist season. Suffice it to say, tourism is important to our economy. And we're **grateful to have you**.

Pleasantries aside, though, you are a guest. So please **act like it**.

Throughout your stay you may be tempted to:

-taunt wild animals.

-stop in the middle of the road.

-scamper off the safe path to get the perfect selfie.

-possibly litter or vandalize.

It doesn't mean you're a terrible person (not to say it couldn't, though), it just means that you are on vacation in a place you don't live and might be tempted to do something stupid or out of character.

We've all been tempted to throw a rock in a mud pot while touring **Yellowstone**, or pet a **bull elk**, but stopping before we do it is well- worth the exercise in discipline. Oh, and just kidding about petting animals. Talk to someone safe if this is a temptation of yours.

Just make good decisions and be respectful of the fact that **this place is amazing.**

...And that the people who live here would really **REALLY** like to keep it that way.

TELEGRAPH ENTRY, 2/22/21

Empathy: Local Roads Want to Know How YOU Are

Winter hit. Finally. Something to do with La Nina & barometers and whatnot. The phenomenon has caused droves of manic citizens to network in order to procure up-to-date road conditions in the area. Taking to such platforms as Powell Valley Exchange, Cody Area Classifieds, and Farmers Only, would-be travelers repeatedly petition for updates as near as the grocery store, to as far away as Billings.

Noticing and feeling complete compassion for the weather detectives, Local Roads want you to know they are wondering the same thing. Only the other way around. Said the Belfry Highway to Telegraph Reporters,

'Honestly, we're concerned about you, too. Ignoring such silly things as road reports, 200mph winds, and several highway cameras in the area can be really taxing on a person. Just stay put, drink some hot cocoa, and know you are loved.'

Aww, thanks, Local Roads. And thanks to the people who also comment. 'is this still available?' to every single non-commerce-related post on social media. Y'all are the real heroes.

Stay warm, and stay off the buy and sell groups until spring.

The Telegraph

TINY CHAPTER 2

CODY-YOUR LIKELY HOME BASE

If you aren't actually staying in **Cody, Wyoming** throughout the duration of your trip, you'll at least be there a time or two. It's a great town whose namesake is **William F. Cody**-better known as **Buffalo Bill** (great showman, miserable conservationist; Google him).

Cody is roughly 50 miles from the **East entrance of Yellowstone**, has an approximate population of 10,000, and touts itself as the **Rodeo Capital of the World.**

Cody is a tourist's dream. Cool places to eat, lots of fun shops, and excellent surrounding scenery. The people are super cool, too. Most everyone is happy to answer questions and make recommendations for maximizing your vacation, so ask around. Sure there are some pretentious people here and there, but even then, they're still pretty cool. Probably aren't natives, either. Just saying.

You'll like **Cody**. **Cody** is like **Jackson Hole**'s less pretentious brother who just wants to see you enjoy yourself...but will probably punch you if you touch his perfect hair. Make sense? Probably not. Especially if you've never been to **Jackson**. Enjoy the place, either way.

Oh. We love you, **Jackson**. It's just. We can't afford to visit. Don't take it personally.

TELEGRAPH SEMI PRO TIPS

- Walk from place to place as much as you can. It's nice out and you won't have to worry about parking. You'll also notice stores and attractions that may have otherwise been overlooked while running a red light in your 300' motorhome.

- Each souvenir shop is both similar and different from the previous. That said, they're all worth a stop.

- Take time to people-watch at the parks. It's fun and often entertaining considering people visit from all over the world, from all walks of life. Just remember: the weirdos are probably tourists, like you. Okay, not *you* you, but you get the idea.

HOW TO IRRITATE THE LOCALS

- Running red lights in your 300' motorhome.

- Being rude at a restaurant. You're on vacation, it's okay if your reservation is running a little behind.

HOW TO GET HURT

- Running red lights in your 300' motorhome.

OTHER TOWNS IN THE BASIN

Much love to the surrounding towns in **Park County**, too. While they don't quite get the traffic that **Cody** does, they're still worth a visit.

POWELL

Around 6000 people, **Powell** is an excellent community to beat the crowds and still take in a lot of what Cody has to offer. Have a burger and beer at **WYOld West Brewing**, an iced something or other from **Uncommon Grounds** or **Gestalt**, or just do some hot laps at **Homesteader Park**. Great **golf course**, too.

Powell has a ton of public land around it. **Polecat Bench** is a quick trip north of town and offers some great opportunities for **hiking** or **mountain biking**. Maybe even a fossil or two. Check your go-to app for trail segments or pay the chamber building a visit for further insights.

CLARK

30 miles north of Cody (HWY120), **Clark** has a population of just over 3000 people- although everyone is spread out enough that you won't be able to tell.

Swing in to **Edelweiss Saloon** for an amazing burger, dip your toes in the beautiful **Clarks Fork River**, and follow **1AB to Canyon Road** for an up-close glimpse at one of the most beautiful vistas in the country: the **Clarks Fork Canyon**.

MEETEETSE

An incredible town! Some 450 residents, **Meeteetse** offers a fantastic view of the **Absarokas**. **Meeteetse** also has some of the best eats in the area. I'm fat so I should know.

Grab breakfast at the **Mercantile** and split lunch and dinner between **The Elkhorn** and **The Cowboy**. You won't be disappointed. Ohh, then top things off with a gaggle of truffles from the **Meeteetse Chocolatier**. They're amazing.

Any additional info on this place will have to be acquired on your own. If we give up too much more, we might get whooped. Same for **Clark**. We love y'all. Please don't beat us up.

TINY CHAPTER 3

RECREATION AND WHATNOT

> "Hey, Stupid. We're wild and we maul stuff."
>
> -the animals

This chapter is the biggest. After all, recreation is why you chose this place-and options for it are aplenty. Depending on the length of your stay and budget, you may have to be strategic on how you fill your time with cool stuff, so here's our two cents:

HIKING

Some people like to cheat death while walking up mountains. Some just prefer a casual stroll through nature without any agenda. The area has opportunities for both.

Consider the **Beck Lake Trail** (desert, lake, easy directions) system or **the Shoshone Riverway Trail** (riverfront, more fertile, flat) for something basic and close to **Cody**. The **Cedar Mountain** (more elevation, trees, possibly wildlife) area is also decent if you're looking for more of a challenge.

If something more terrifying is what you're after, there are several trailheads along the **North Fork Highway** (HWY 14-the one you take to **Yellowstone**) that will more than suffice. The terrain and difficulty on these trails are endless, which is exactly why we won't list them here. Sure you can Google them or pick up a map, but allow us to make the case for planning with a professional.

While no trail around **Cody** is perfectly without risk, these bigger trails are especially dangerous if you don't know what you're doing. That includes you, Tad.

We all know you've done a **Spartan Race**, but you're no match for getting lost in the **Absaroka Mountains**. For real. Just accept it. Humility is attractive.

For the bigger hikes, know they exist. Start by speaking to someone at **Sunlight Sports** (the owner has literally written an entire book on hiking around here. Buy it). They know the right questions to ask and can get you safely set up for what you're after. Don't forget urban hiking from shop to shop is also entertaining and much less likely to introduce you to a bear.

TELEGRAPH SEMI PRO TIPS

- Take your earbuds out. Not only does nature sound amazing, you'll never hear danger approaching with Dua Lipa squelching in your ears.

- Listen for the rattle of snakes, they will ruin any hike, if given the opportunity.

- NEVER hike alone and ALWAYS carry bear spray.

- Know how to use bear spray. Watch a video on YouTube. Have a plan.

- Plan on losing cell phone service, even if you have it when you start your hike. That said, ALWAYS let someone know where you'll be.

- Bring water.

HOW TO IRRITATE THE LOCALS

- Pack it in, pack it out, yo. Littering automatically makes you a bad person. It's non-negotiable.

- Bikers yield to hikers, everyone yields to horses.

HOW TO GET HURT

- Don't overestimate your experience level. You will surely get hurt.

BIKING

Bikes are great. Especially **mountain bikes**. Especially – *especially* – when going downhill. Much the same rules apply to riding a bike as they do hiking (safety, skill level, having a plan), while the risk-to- reward margin is off the charts. Again with the bias, but the **Bighorn Basin** (what the cool people call this area) has some of the best mountain biking in the country when things like accessibility, variety, community, and sustainability are all considered holistically.

It is **The Telegraph's** own opinion that all the riding you could ever fancy is very close to **Cody**. Or should we say, you don't need to travel far to ride rad stuff. This is the second plug for the **Beck Lake Trail** system. Easy climbs, then descents for every skill level and style of riding. Beck is an excellent trail system that also includes a terrain park, jump lines, and even a pump track. There's a paved track around the reservoir, if that's your jam, on wheel or foot, as well. Trail maps exist at every major trail junction.

After you've worn out **Beck**, consider a quick trip North of **Cody** to the **Outlaw Trail** system. Heading north on the **Belfry Highway** (HWY 120), t urn west at the **Cody Shooting Complex** sign and follow the road for a ways after it turns to gravel. Parking isn't anything special, and you do have to (legally) hop a fence, but the

Outlaw stuff is the real deal. Check **Strava** for segments if you're still having troubles finding the place.

If you get sick of **Outlaw**, you're either sponsored or a liar. No matter which of the two, stop at **Joyvagen Bicycle Shop** to discuss more spots to shred. They're cool people and also rent bikes, should you be successful at talking your weird uncle into riding with you on vacation.

> **Note**: road cycling is also amazing around here. We'll trust you pretty much know where those trails are. Summer months in **Cody** country can make for busy highways so be extremely careful and consider riding as early as possible before the mob hits.

TELEGRAPH SEMI PRO TIPS

- Same deal with the earbuds. Keep them out. The sound of a freewheeling mountain bike is sweeter than string music.

- Bring water. Then bring a little more if it's hot. There's a decent amount of desert where you're shredding-just play it safe.

- Even though you are close to town, make sure people know where you are and when they can expect you home.

- Consider gravel riding as a way to get your road fix AND hear the magic sound of a bike tire on hard dirt-the traffic will also be less. Talk to Joyvagen if this is the first time you've heard of gravel.

HOW TO IRRITATE THE LOCALS

- The Telegraph is a staunch proponent of 'share the road.' That said, remember you are still smaller than a truck whose driver might not be so great at sharing. Good etiquette on the trail and the road go a long- ways towards staying safe and keeping the peace.

HOW TO GET HURT

- Assuming you are more important than everyone else will get you hurt. So will not wearing a helmet.

- If you are riding a trail for the first time, do it cautiously. Once you have a feel for it, then you can shred.

TRAIL RIDES AND DRIVES

So self-propelled locomotion might not be your thing. That's cool. You may prefer to ride atop large mammals or upon motorized thingys as a means of covering ground like a mounted warrior. Well, **Cody** country has a fix for that, Mad Max.

Again, with the assumptions, but we'll go ahead and say you probably didn't check your horses on the airplane? Or if you did bring them, we'll boldly posit that since you own horses you know what you're doing and where you're going. Fair? Hopefully that's fair.

For everyone else, you need to enlist the help of a guide. We wish there was more of a surprise. There isn't. There are guides close to Cody like **Cedar Mountain Trail Rides**, as well as, most of the guest ranches on your way to **Yellowstone**. Some guest ranches require you to be staying with them, others do not. Call ahead. No real revelations here, folks. Trail rides are pretty cut and dry.

If gasoline is your adrenaline drug of choice, pay **Tread 'n' Trails** a visit on the west end of **Cody**. They rent several different types of **UTV**s-even those paved-road ones that look like pod racers. Not completely sure what **UTV** stands for? **Utility Terrain Vehicles**, that's what. Think 'side by side'. They're super rad and can go just about anywhere, which makes for another great option to take this place in. The staff is great and maps come standard.

TELEGRAPH SEMI PRO TIPS

- Wear a Kid Rock shirt when driving a UTV, it'll just feel right.

HOW TO IRRITATE THE LOCALS

- Nothing is more annoying than a moron in a UTV. Save it for the hills, Mario Kart.

HOW TO GET HURT

- Driving your UTV like Mario Kart. You'll end up buying it, too.

- Messing with your horse on a trail ride. If the horse doesn't bite you, your guide will.

FISHING

Understand this, disciples. You stand at the foot of hallowed waters in **Cody** country; Blue ribbon fisheries we simply do not deserve as mortals. There are many types of fish in our waters, but it is the **trout** that rules them all like a god king.

Rainbows, Cutthroats, Browns, Brook, Tiger. Our **trout** are perfect predators. Ghostly harbingers of the **river**. They are beautiful. Profound. One touch and you will seek golden scales as **Gollum** sought the ring. You will wake from sound slumber in a cold sweat. If one of these warriors entertains your attempt to catch them, consider yourself kissed by an angel. Handle the fish here as if they are a stick of dynamite without a waterproof fuse: gently, with an emphasis on getting them in the water as soon as possible.

The headwaters of the **Shoshone River** start just beneath heaven (not like the Slayer song) and continue through **Cody**, **Powell**, and **Lovell** before dumping into the **Bighorn River**. There is public access in **Cody** along the **Shoshone Riverway Trail**, as well as, beneath the **Corbett Bridge,** if you want to try your luck.

The **North Fork** (remember, that's the highway you take to Yellowstone) of the **Shoshone River** is a bit of a drive but also offers some great trout fishing. There is plenty of access along the highway, just watch for bears.

Beck Lake and **Cody Reservoir** offer family friendly options to cast a worm or spinner if that is more along the lines of what you're after. **Buffalo Bill Reservoir** is also an option, but fishing from the shore can be frustrating-especially if the wind is blowing. Speaking of wind, **Buffalo Bill Reservoir** gets extremely dangerous for smaller watercraft when it blows. Don't take the raft you just bought at Wal-Mart out on this water. Ever. Same goes for you and your paddle board, Lisa.

It is the manic recommendation of **The Telegraph** that you speak to a guide service before you venture out. Furthermore, actually paying for a guided float will not let you down in the least. It is by far the best way to experience our water. Pay **Wyoming Trout Guides** a visit if you're on the fence. They'll give you some options and you can decide from there. One stroll through their Facebook page and you'll throw money at them like Nolan Ryan.

TELEGRAPH SEMI PRO TIPS

- You'll need a fishing license, pilgrim. You and everyone in your party older than 14. Don't cheat this one.

- Forgive the elitism, but use a fly rod. It'll change your life.

- Pay. For. A. Guide.

- Grab a set of regulations to see where closures are and what limits are.

- Treble hooks rarely bode well for a trout. Leave those for the bass.

- Also, bend your barbs down. See 'How to Irritate the Locals' for further guidance on catch and release.

HOW TO IRRITATE THE LOCALS

- Wandering onto private property would do the trick.

- Keeping a fish just so you can bring it back and show your significant other is wasteful. If you have the means to clean and eat it-and if regulations allow-go for it. They're delicious. Otherwise take a quick pic and get it back in the water. Catch and release doesn't guarantee a fish will survive, but the odds are sharply better than taking it back to your hotel.

HOW TO GET HURT

It's water. Be careful. Bring a PFD. Wear the PFD. *Not to be confused with .pdf

Believe it or not, animals that can maul you also love the river. It is not uncommon for bears or mountain lions to visit, so, again with the Bear Spray. It is never a bad idea.

CAMPING

Note that header, **camping** not glamping. For those of you that navigate the 300' land yachts to and fro, the myriad of RV parks, **Ponderosa Campground, Cody KOA, etc**, your plans and docking stations can be secured but should be reserved as space is limited. We appreciate your patronage and congratulate you on your material success as only ten wheels and five slide-outs can display, but this particular section of this handbook may not apply as parking space is less than expected.

The **Shoshone National Forest** provides 20 official **campgrounds** (South Fork of the Shoshone, North Fork of the Shoshone, Meeteetse area, and the Beartooth Plateau) that may accommodate more modern camping/glamping sites fit for driven or towed means of pseudo off-grid living. Some of these **campsites** may provide power and/or dump stations but don't count on it, after all you are venturing into one of the last, truly wild spaces in the lower 48. **Campground hosts** will be a great resource when reserving and inhabiting developed spaces along any of these thoroughfares. Please remember you are choosing to park in **bear country** and personal security (bear spray) and **campground safety** (responsible food storage) should always be at the forefront of your outdoor experience.

For those of you with an adventurous spirit and desire for the full **wilderness** experience, **Park County** includes north of 3.5 million acres of **BLM** and **U.S. Forest Service managed land**, commonly referred to as **Public Land**. Accessed by well marked trailheads and/or county roads these lands allow for tent, tarp, and/or camper inhabitants to truly embrace the great American legacy of public lands, free of charge. They are there for you to enjoy but keep in mind that you are not fond of your neighbors tossing their **garbage** on your **porch** at home, so please leave your chosen spaces **better than when you arrived**.

There are no reservations required but there are a few guidelines that should be followed to ensure we all may enjoy these spaces today and in the generations to come. If the full DIY experience intimidates you, many **local outfitters** can provide a truly five-star backcountry experience with appropriate planning and notice.

TELEGRAPH SEMI PRO TIPS

- DIY on US Forest Service Land and BLM managed lands allows for 14 day camping limits, if planning on staying longer than that you're to move five miles from your initial site

- Pack it in, pack it out.

- If you're looking to avoid an intense camping trip in tents, hang your food 100 yards from where you sleep or use a bear box (if available). There are critters here that like the smells of what we all like to eat.

- You are in the Rocky Mountains and snow in July is not an absurd occurrence, prepare accordingly

- Dispersed camping means what it says, 200' off trails and away from lakes and 100' off of streams or creeks, this goes for your natural waste as well. Dig a hole and cover it or pack it out with you. No one wants to step in recycled freeze dried meals.

- Bear spray is your wilderness seatbelt, better to have it and not need it than to need it and wished you would've had it.

HOW TO IRRITATE THE LOCALS

- Rocks and trees existed without your initials or signatures before your visit, there's no need to leave a mark, take the selfie rather than scar the landscape

- We live and recreate here all year, please leave the place like you found it.

- If the night is cold and a fire is required, be sure to drown the coals before you leave. Smokey the Bear nailed things years ago, "Only you can prevent forest fires!"

HOW TO GET HURT

- Sleeping with your snacks will get you hurt. Bears are the land version of sharks, they have a sense of smell 2,100 times better than we do. Your midnight snack is an open invitation to becoming a midnight snack.

- Snow in the Rocky Mountains can be a monthly occurrence, plan for the nitty gritty and enjoy when it spares you.

- Venturing into the wild without letting someone know is also a good way to get hurt. 3.5 million acres is 5x the size of Rhode Island. We want you to return home safely more than you may know.

YELLOWSTONE

The Big Dance. Nirvana. Top of the mountain. The hip **caldera** everyone is talking about. The first, greatest, and probably the most [potentially] deadly **national park** in these great **United States**. YELLOWSTONE!

One of the largest **calderas** in the world, which is just a fancy way of saying 'massive crater left after a catastrophic volcanic eruption', **Yellowstone** sprawls some 3400 square miles. According to their website, 96% of **Yellowstone** exists in **Wyoming**-which is appropriate, because **Wyoming is 100% the greatest territory on the planet.**

Just don't move here. Bears, remember?

Quite evidently, **Yellowstone** is still very much volcanically active. Probably the reason you and four million other people made the trip. Geothermal heat from beneath **Yellowstone** accounts for all those rad, smelly thermal features you intend to visit-which account for thousands of dads being wrongly accused of making (the stink part).

There are five entrances to the **park**. You will probably take the **East Entrance**, as it's a straight shot from **Cody**. Think of **Yellowstone** as a big, weird loop. Whether you go left or right after **Fishing Bridge**, you'll eventually make your way back-provided that's your intended route.

There are a million things we could list about **Yellowstone**, but that would take too long. Consider these Semi Pro Tips as a consolation prize.

TELEGRAPH SEMI PRO TIPS

- The Norris Geyser Basin and Canyon are must-stops. Consider Lamar Valley, Firehole, Grand Prismatic, and Mammoth, too. Basically the entire park.

- Fishing Bridge, Canyon, Norris, Madison, Old Faithful, and Grant Village are the six main info sites on the big loop. If you have the time, they are worth a stop.

- West Yellowstone and Albright visitor centers are a ways off the beaten path, but are still great to see

- MOST of the roads through Yellowstone are pretty narrow. You will struggle in a 300' motorhome. If you have the means, tour the park in a smaller vehicle.

- Stop and dip your toes in Yellowstone Lake. It's pretty fantastic.

- You CAN fish select places in Yellowstone. You need an additional permit that can be purchased from most of the visitor centers-Fishing Bridge, Canyon, and Grant Village, for sure.

- Most of the big attractions have hiking trails. Take the time to walk them. There are fewer people the further you go, and you will see some bonus material.

HOW TO IRRITATE THE LOCALS

- EVERYONE wants to stop and watch wildlife from the side of the road. If there's room, great, pull over. If there isn't room, keep going until you find some. Stopping dead in the middle of the road is not only rude, but pretty dangerous.

- Read and understand the regulations. Things that are found in the park stay in the park.

- No littering. The point of the park is to preserve it. As is.

- Do not put a baby bison in your car. It has been done. It is not a good idea.

HOW TO GET HURT

- Do not approach wildlife. They will charge, maim, and possibly kill you.

- Do not step off the boardwalk. Some surfaces around the boardwalk are thin enough for you to fall through and get blanched like a tomato. Believe us when we say tourists get hurt every year for breaking the rules in the park. Whether for your safety, or the park's safety, follow the rules.

- Google accidents in Yellowstone if you're still a skeptic.

TELEGRAPH ENTRY, 2/22/21

<u>CHUD Discovered in COVID-Free Sewers.</u>

These days, it seems there's always a trade with good news. Perhaps no finer example exists than Park County's initial discovery that COVID-19 was not present in early sewage samples. It basically means one of two things: as it stands, exposure in the Basin has remained low...or people with the virus do not use toilets. Lets hope it's the first option.

Here's the bad news: they did find C.H.U.D. Yep. Cannibalistic Humanoid Underground Dwellers are pretty rampant in our sewers, it turns out. Baffled, a representative with the sewer task force explained the following initial steps to The Telegraph,

'Honestly, we're stumped. We do know that CHUD leave the elderly and immunocompromised alone, so at least they can finally catch a break. Plus, at least CHUD are big enough to shoot.'

Why couldn't it have been Ninja Turtles?! We just don't know. For now, we'll just take the small victory of no COVID in the sewer and rest in the fact that CHUD can be shot.

Hang in there,

The Telegraph

TINY CHAPTER 4

OTHER ACTIVITIES

Yellowstone/Cody country has so much to offer. There is no qualifying criteria as to what made this guide and what didn't, other than to say what has been listed up to this point satisfies the most obvious of choices. If you've been disappointed thus far, take heart in knowing, that as far as tourist-y purchases, this one is among the more affordable. Use the pages as kindling for your legal campfires if you need, that will provide some retribution.

Alas, whether you love or hate what you've learned thus far, the remaining activities are the honorable mentions to consider if your budget, spirit of adventure, or schedules still allow. Read on, warriors. Read on.

SLEEPING GIANT ZIPLINE

Sleeping Giant is a success story. The mountain had closed its doors a while ago due to financial strife not uncommon to a ski mountain. Locals mourned the loss after fighting to keep the place operational. following a brief period of dormancy, a **Cody** native purchased the mountain with the lofty goal of transforming it into a multi-season destination worthy of the most lit of thrill seekers. Goal accomplished. Welcome to the **zipline**, folks.

A Tripadvisor badge on **Sleeping Giant**'s website places the **zipline** at number three of 36 outdoor activities in the **Cody** area. We're no mathematicians, but that's a pretty solid placement. Professionally designed and built, the **zipline** boasts speeds of 45 miles per hour for some participants. While these eyelid-peeling speeds are completely safe, they will satisfy the adrenalin junkies in your family-perhaps even leaving a bug or two in their teeth. SELFIE!

Sleeping Giant is very pro-community and often partners with various organizations throughout the **Basin** to host events. Show them some love and book a **zipline** trip. For best results, use their online booking tool at zipsg.com.

TELEGRAPH SEMI PRO TIPS

- Take a fly rod. You drive along the North Fork of the Shoshone River for most of the trip.

- Everyone likes a cold beer in the mountains. Wait until you're done, though. There's plenty alternate beverages for the littles to drink, as well.

- Do what they tell you at the zipline. You have to for your safety, but it also makes everything go much more harmoniously if you willingly comply.

HOW TO IRRITATE THE LOCALS

- Tough to do up there. That's not a challenge, they're just good people. Follow the rules and respect the land. East Peasey.

HOW TO GET HURT

- Ignore what they tell you.

GUNS AND SUCH

This is the Wild West, peeps. It might not be your particular lifestyle, but you have to admit, there's something you like about this place besides the views. The public land? Maybe. The people? Hopefully. The activities? Obviously. The fact that **firearms** are everywhere in a completely normal way? Yeah? Then stay with us. No? Still stay with us.

Now, the second amendment is a bit of a touchy subject for some. Maybe you love it. You may even have a respectable collection you fancy using regularly. Excellent. Welcome. You'll make a lot of friends here.

Maye you don't like **firearms**. Maybe they make you nervous. Maybe you think they're only for zealots out of touch with modern society? Maybe the only thing you know about **firearms** is what you're told on primetime. To each their own. We aren't here to be your moral compass. BUT. You're on vacation and have the opportunity to learn about them in a healthy, professional, and completely safe fashion. Shouldn't you at least find out for yourself? You should. Do it, Brince!

Regardless of your personal stance, **Cody Firearms Experience** is a one-of-a-kind chance to experience these sophisticated instruments the way they are intended. To be educated on how to correctly handle and operate one by legitimate professionals.

'From flintlock to full auto' as their website states, **Cody Firearms Experience** allows you to discharge **firearms** of all types. SAFELY and CORRECTLY by PROFESSIONALS. Yeah, they even have a Gatling Gun.

Start with their website to book your experience, or give them a call if you have any questions beforehand. Don't say we didn't warn you about a great time!

TELEGRAPH SEMI PRO TIPS

- Sure the Gatling Gun or the M-16 are a must, but take time with an old Colt revolver or Henry. The classics are always timeless.

- Check your expectations at the door, good or bad. Be a part of the firearms experience.

- Smile. For real. Especially if you didn't think you would. We get it.

HOW TO IRRITATE THE LOCALS

- If you still aren't convinced by the operation of a firearm, try to respectfully entertain why others are. You're welcome to evangelize against them around here, but brush up on your humility, beforehand.

HOW TO GET HURT

- Do exactly as you're told by your instructor, and the odds of injury will be lower than just about anything else you'll do during your trip.

STAMPEDE

Rodeos. Parades. Music. Fireworks, and more! Finding yourself in **Cody** country on or around **Independence Day** may very well be the best tourist experience available. You will literally be drinking the **Cody** experience from a fire hose for five days. Kicking off with the **Yellowstone Extreme Bulls** event on June 30th and followed nightly by **Professional Rodeo Cowboys Association (PRCA)** sanctioned events July 1st through the 4th, you'll quickly understand the deserved title of **"Rodeo Capital of the World."**

If ropin' and ridin' are not your thing but people watching is, July 2nd marks the first of three **parades** wherein the community, surrounding area and state of **Wyoming** showcase our culture and lifestyles. The city park is buzzing with free concerts daily and in the farmer's market style, local food and craft vendors keep you fed and supporting the local economy without leaving the downtown area.

The celebration truly goes all day and night as many of the local watering holes operate with extended hours allowing for the opportunity to socialize, indulge and dance at all hours. The **free fireworks** show (they are set off north of the river on the west side of town on the evening of the 4th) will leave you in awe and full of an American spirit of independence. The only excuse for boredom during the Stampede is your choice to stay inside.

TELEGRAPH SEMI PRO TIPS

- Be ready to fight for space on the sidewalks to watch the parade. Especially if you want shade. Parking is pretty much impossible, so plan to walk.

- Walk around the vendor booths near the park. There are some incredible local artisans, there. Good food, too.

HOW TO IRRITATE THE LOCALS

- You'll irritate us by fighting too much for the good parade spots. Many locals put out a bunch of chairs the night before. Touch them and you may be punched by a mom or dad suffering from heatstroke. Just saying.

HOW TO GET HURT

- Leave the parade horses alone. Don't let your kids run out into the street, either. The outriders take this seriously and are not to be trifled with.

MUSEUMS

Museums. There are a bunch around here. Big, small, niche, we got 'em. Escape the heat and check them out.

THE BUFFALO BILL CENTER OF THE WEST

With any serious effort to plan your trip to **Yellowstone**, you've surely heard of the **Buffalo Bill Center of the West**. The museum's footprint sprawls along Eighth Street (Sheridan Avenue, really. You can't miss it.) and should not be left off your planner.

There are five museums at the Center:

- **Buffalo Bill Museum**
  - American West-type stuff, including all things William F. Cody.

- **Plains Indian Museum**
  - There is much in this handbook about us 'locals'. That's a misnomer. The Plains Indians museum plays homage to the native people of these lands, and should not be overlooked. The collection will rival anything you've seen elsewhere.

- **Cody Firearms Museum**
  - There are 10,000 artifacts, here. Enough said.

- **Draper Natural History Museum**
    - A fascinating look at Yellowstone's ecosystem. Your kids will like this one.
- **Whitney Western Art Museum**
    - Western art galore. Even if you don't consider yourself an art buff.

You should budget the better part of a day to get anywhere near the end of this place. Have a plan if you intend to bring your littles-they may not appreciate Western art as much as you, and the other patrons might not appreciate that they don't appreciate Western art. Make sense?

Other super rad museums to consider:

- **Cody Dug Up Gun Museum**
    - More guns! Totally different vibe than the BBCW. That isn't good or

bad, but it does mean this place is worth a stop.

- **Buffalo Bill Dam & Visitor Center**

  ○ Tons of opportunities to say 'dam'. This place is pretty fascinating, especially considering how vital the dam is to our basin.

- **By Western Hands Museum & Gallery**

  ○ More guild-style, highlighting the West-past and present. They host workshops from time to time, as well. Free admission!

- **Cody Heritage Museum**

  ○ Just as the name states. A pretty cool place to learn about Cody.

- **Heart Mountain WWII Interpretive Center**

- The sobering history behind one of the Basin's most recognizable landmarks. This place is a bit of a drive from Cody.

- **Historic Cody Mural and Museum**
  - See the Grigware mural up close and personal for an idea of what the Basin looked like to settlers.

- **Homesteader Museum**
  - A quaint, entertaining slice of our history-loaded to the ceiling with cool artifacts and photos. This museum is in Powell and is one of a kind. Worth the trip. Plan to stay in Powell all day for smaller crowds, good eats and cool stores.

- **Meeteetse Museums**
  - A three-in-one stop (includes the Charles Belden Museum of Western

Photography and the Bank Museum) dedicated to the history of this awesome town-about a half hour south of Cody. Grab a burger from the Elkhorn and some truffles from the Meeteetse Chocolatier, too.

RIVER RAFTING

That hallowed water we spoke of in the fishing chapter? Well here's another opportunity for baptism, disciples! **River Rafting** has been **Cody's** number one outdoor activity since 2012, according to Tripadvisor, so get to it.

The **Shoshone River** is public property from shore to shore-it is also your go-to water for the float of a lifetime. While the water is public, you can't anchor where it flows through private land, or pull over for a stroll (sorry, this includes potty breaks). It is what it is.

So now that you know the rule, it's time to buy an inner tube and float, right? Meh... probably not on your own. Just because you can doesn't mean you should- especially if you are unfamiliar with the area (including public take-outs).

You won't see **Shoshone River** rapids on the Red Bull tour, but there is enough white water (you'll get wet. No, soaked) that you are far better off-you guessed it- hiring a guide.

TELEGRAPH SEMI PRO TIPS

- It kind of goes without saying, but don't take anything that isn't waterproof. If you absolutely cannot part with your celly, make sure it stays tethered to you in a protective case. Consider a GoPro if pictures/video are all you want-cell service sucks on most sections of the river.

HOW TO IRRITATE THE LOCALS

- You should be good under the supervision of a guide.

- There's time for chitchat on the boat, but no one cares what you think about politics, Susan. Quiet coyote.

HOW TO GET HURT

- Same. Do what your guide tells you. There's risk involved with everything, but your rafting trip is pretty safe if you make good decisions.

TELEGRAPH ENTRY, 9/8/21

Local Farm & Ranch Supplier Now Offering Ivermectin Smoothies

Conspiracy abounds surrounding the efficacy of Ivermectin to treat COVID.

Stalling endorsement for a rushed FDA approval of vaccines? Maybe. Another reason for the left to loathe hillbillies? Also maybe. Big pharma's appetite for raking in money? Also also maybe.

One thing is for sure-in spite of all the hullabaloo: the situation makes for a great smoothie. Said a marketing rep for a local Park County Farm and Ranch Store,

'Whether or not it works to treat COVID, I think we can all agree that

a little apple-flavored Ivermectin blended with kiwi and acai makes for a fantastic afternoon pick-me-up'.

No arguments, here. After all, Main and Tail shampoo has long been used on human heads for richer, fuller hair. And that's pretty much the same thing. Right?

-The Telegraph

POORLY DEFINED (AND DRAWN) THINGS

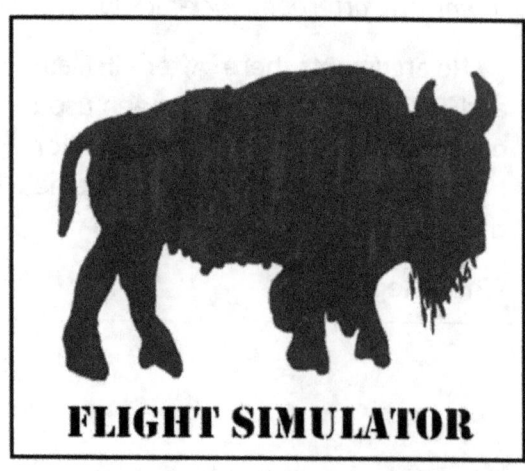

FLIGHT SIMULATOR

This is an Abrahams Tank covered in fur. With horns. They look big and clumsy until the very second they've had enough of your crap. They also don't care what you placed at state in the 400, Liz. You take one more selfie and you'll hit orbit quicker than a tech billionaire.

URSUS ATTACTOS

These 10,000-pound apex predators have no patience for your cheeky attempts to taunt them. Even if it's from a mile away. No, Garrett, they aren't spiritually connecting with you, either. They're tasting you from afar to see if it's worth the effort. Lucky for you, you probably taste like beer and chewing tobacco.

MURDER FOUNTAIN

These things shoot a gazillion gallons of water that is over 200 degrees Fahrenheit. Your flesh will be blanched from your body like a tomato, should you try to look rebellious and approach. No, Julie. The mineral water won't help your enlarged pores.

LITERALLY ANYTHING STEAMING

These are fumaroles. They are like angry, smelly, rock-anuses that blow steam and hydrogen sulfide gas-both of which can kill you. Don't be a funny guy, Chad. You plugging your nose by one with a frown pretending you tooted isn't that funny of a picture. Be a better example to your children.

BUGLE NINJA

Another massive mammal with the capacity to impale you. Just because they may let you get close, doesn't mean they won't antler-stab you like an assassin. Sure, Tim, you're an expert from the interwebs on big game, though. You know how to handle these bad boys, right?

BOILING PONDS

Ever see that famous movie about the volcano? Where the couple gets frisky in a mineral pool? These things will scald you to death and then digest your body like a Mentos in Coke. Stay away and say no to PDA. You have a rented motorhome, fool around in there.

BOARDWALK EDGELORDING

These picturesque bridges exist for more than, 'finding the new me' posts on Instagram, Becky. In some places within Yellowstone, the walking surfaces can be very thin and brittle, and the boardwalks were built to keep you safe. Swallow your shallow sense of adventure and stay on the boardwalk. Because if you fall through being an idiot-yep-cooked like a lobster.

INGLORIOUS BUZZTERD

We have one venomous snake in Wyoming. It's pretty bashful up until you stray too close. Then it gets pissed and rattles. Only the rattle sounds like a buzz. The snake is trying to tell you it wants to be left alone. When you try to play Crocodile Hunter, that's when it strikes at you in front of your friends. At which point you lose your feeble temper and kill the snake. Just keep walking if you see one. There will never be another Crocodile Hunter-especially not you, bro.

More myth than material, Belk stands as The Telegraph's flagship mascot. The sum total of all you laugh and cry at, love and hate, fear and embrace. Your lucid thoughts divided by forgetfulness.

Confidence multiplied by insecurity. Interest earned on good decisions pickpocketed by bad ones. Belk is peaceful, yet warmongering. You may not see Belk-but Belk sees you, friend. Believe, anyway.

Same drama as Belk. Trout with antlers just look super cool. Buy lots of merchandise, consumer!

TELEGRAPH ENTRY, 11/18/19

Wyoming Barley Grower Pens Sultry Memoir, '50 Shades of Grain'

Reader Discretion Advised

Big news on the literary front from right here in the Big Horn Basin. A mysterious author who goes by the pen name, E. L. Maltnasty has taken our prudent community by storm after announcing the release his haughty farming memoir, '50 Shades of Grain.' The adult-themed publication is a collection of short stories involving the naughtier side of raising grain in Wyoming. The following excerpt, in particular, had our review team blushing:

'I Throttled my Gleaner through acres of Moravian 69, a sassy two-row

variety. The blonde stalks needed a real good threshing, and I was just the guy. Chaff was everywhere. Those golden kernels were practically malting themselves....'

Too hot for TV. Too hot for The Telegraph. That's all for now, puritans.

-The Telegraph

WORTHLESS MAPS

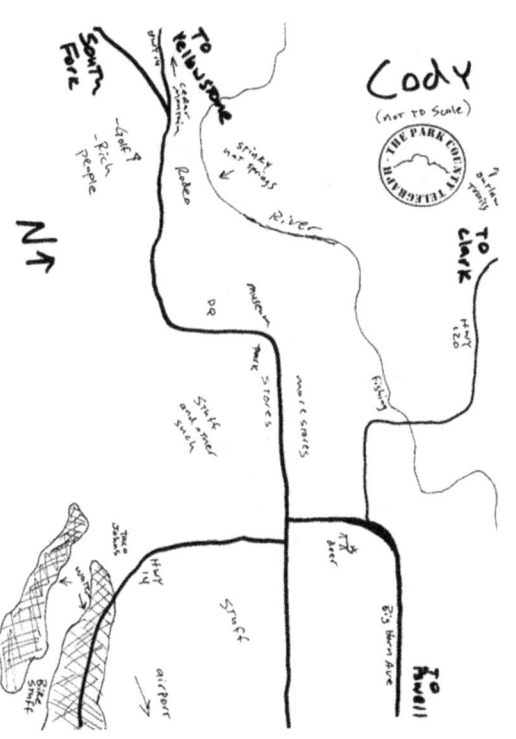

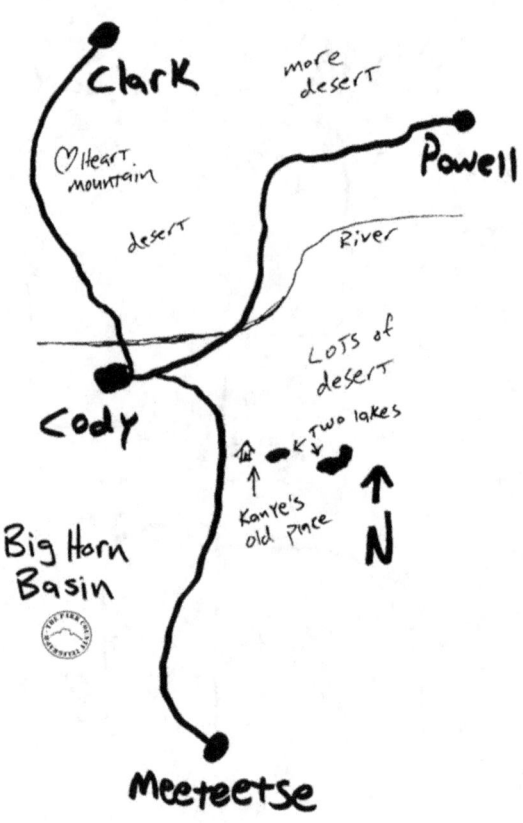

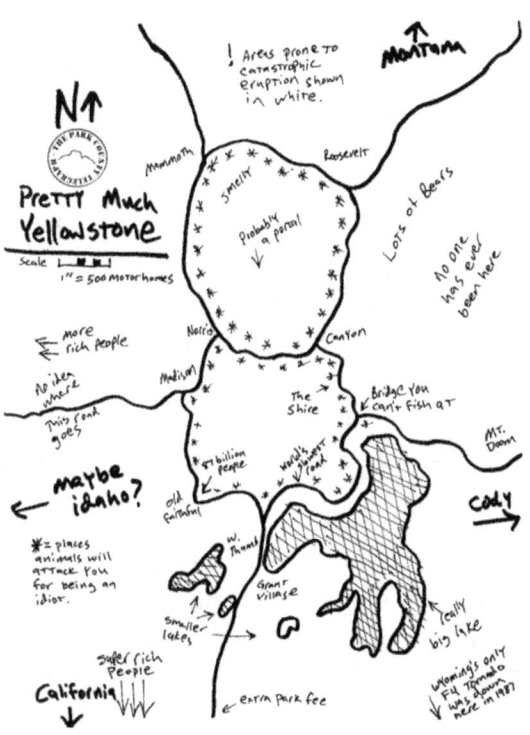

TELEGRAPH ENTRY, 5/5/20

Wyoming Upland Enthusiasts Eager for Murder Hornet Season

Its springtime in Park County! Crops are being planted, trees are getting leaves, and Ringneck Pheasants are scampering everywhere! At times, you'd barely even notice the entire world has ground to a halt like a fat kid falling off a skateboard. Ahh, yes. Spring.

Not to be outdone by some ball-hog of a pandemic, the animal kingdom has decided to release the Kraken of winged insects on American soil: The Murder Hornet. Native to Asia (Wuhan, we're pretty sure), the harbinger of death has thankfully made its way stateside. Making the best out of a bad situation like they always do, Wyoming folk have come up with a solution...blow them away with a shotgun. Said a local upland hunter to The Telegraph,

'Actually, it's not all bad. We'll just blow these winged bastards away with a friggin' twelve gauge. Should really help dial us in for Chukar season. Might even try to breast 'em out and smoke 'em.'

How to we love thee, Wyoming? let us count the ways! Pull those scatterguns out of summer retirement and get ready for the onslaught. We all need a bit of an escape after being quarantined for months.

Happy Hunting from The Telegraph!

JANKY GAMES

```
K R T Z C A L D E R A R B B Y
A L H R U A E L K J M S X E W
H S E S T Z E G H I N E L N V
Y T R R T Z S F E P O L T X U
D L M T H H Y B C Q O F S R E
R N O L R K E A D W P I Q V Z
O E P N O D G P S R O E I T I
G D H S A M F T C S L S K S L
E H I C T A O E A T N B J I A
N Y L A U N L N T E G E H R D
S Z E L E G R A P H F L I U A
U H I D Y M T X T U V K E O V
L O E E L O E Y S R W C D T T
F E A D E N I R E V L O W S N
I S M E L L Y D A D X Z Z C O
D G Y L Z Z I R G H Y Y T A D
E T N E D R E T Z Z U B A T B
```

TRELK   TELEGRAPH   CUTTHROAT   SCALDED
BELK   THERMOPHILE   TOURIST   WOLVERINE
GEYSER   YELLOWSTONE   EXPENSIVE   SELFIE
HYDROGEN SULFIDE   CALDERA   DON'T VANDALIZE
GRIZZLY   TAD   SCAT   BUZZTERD   SMELLY DAD

Y E L L O

SAW FUMAROLE	SPENT TOO MUCH	WENT TO MUSEUM	YELLED AT PARENT	HIKED
TALKED TO LOCAL	FISHED	TOOK MODEST SELFIE	SAW B.BILL COSPLAY	SAW ELK
ZIPLINE	DIDN'T VANDALIZE	THE PARK COUNTY TELEGRAPH	SAW RODEO	SAW GEYSER
MADE GOOD DECISION	DIDN'T DRINK TOO MUCH	TAGGED TELEGRAPH ON SOCIAL	WRONG TURN	LOST CELL SERVICE
YELLED AT KIDS	SAW GRIZZLY	DIDN'T LITTER	BIKED	WAS NICE TO WAIT STAFF

ACROSS:
1. NOT GLAMPING
2. MONOGAMOUS GEYSER
3. NOT FOR EDGELORDING
4. WORTHLESS MAP ORIENTATION
5. YOU: _____ MONEY ON TELEGRAPH MERCH
6. NECESSARY AFTER BEING GORED
7. HOT SPRING BACTERIA
8. ONLY ON A LEASH
9. CHEMICAL SYMBOL FOR HYDROGEN SULFIDE
10. MAGOATS
11. FUNNIEST BLOG EVER
12. _____ THE WARNING SIGNS
13. DIFFICULTY OF MAKING CROSSWORD PUZZLE

DOWN:
1. ABBREVIATION FOR TROUT TYPE
2. 300' DEATHMOBILE
3. GEORGE CLINTON, NOT CUSSWORD
4. PEOPLE SOUTH OF YELLOWSTONE
5. VANDALISM IS NOT
6. 50 SHADES OF _____ MEMOIR
7. TRIBE AND RIVER
8. ONLY WHEN AND WHERE ALLOWED
9. LOVING MOUNTAIN W/'O' AT THE END BECAUSE I MESSED UP
10. IMPORTANT PARKING PERCEPTION
11. THOMAS' HOMAGE
12. USED TO LIVE SOUTH OF CODY
13. TYPE OF BUZZTERD

ACKNOWLEDGEMENTS

So it was way harder to write a sort-of-real, sort-of-fake handbook than I had originally anticipated. The following were instrumental in the process. I'm going to write it the way bands used to give credit inside the sleeve of a cassette. Because it looks cool. And because this might be the first and only chance to do as such.

Thanks to the good Lord for the gift of Wyoming. Thanks to Adam Teten for authoring sections of the book, including Camping and Stampede. And for getting me creatively unstuck. He's way smarter and manlier than I am. Thanks to Trudi for proofreading this dumpster fire. I kept many of the follies on purpose out of rebellion to proper prose. Don't blame her. Rebecca for the patience and encouragement. Myranda and Sleepy G for the confidence to market this sort of thing-and for always sharing The Telegraph's stuff. Erin and Gestalt-a creator convincing me to create. And for always indulging my ideas. Dustin and the DSE clan for services second to none. Doug the GOAT for the inspiration to write- especially self-deprecatingly funny stuff. Thomas for the push and belief in my capability. Insomnia for the brainstorming and writing opportunities. The Telegraph's followers for being modest in population but great in benevolence. Anyone reading this. Jessi for her longstanding fandom and support of my silly ideas. For trusting me to spend a small fortune on publishing. And for being super hot. I love you.

-Ben

www.ingramcontent.com/pod-product-compliance
Lightning Source LLC
LaVergne TN
LVHW011846060526
838200LV00054B/4186